THE GOSPEL AND THE PLAYGROUND

The Gospel and the Playground

Reading the Gospel of Mark Using Jewish, Palestinian, and Argentine Children's Poetry

OSVALDO D. VENA

Foreword by Dong Hyeon Jeong

WIPF & STOCK · Eugene, Oregon

THE GOSPEL AND THE PLAYGROUND
Reading the Gospel of Mark Using Jewish, Palestinian,
and Argentine Children's Poetry

Wipf & Stock
An Imprint of Wipf and Stock Publishers
199 W. 8th Ave., Suite 3
Eugene, OR 97401

www.wipfandstock.com

PAPERBACK ISBN: 979-8-3852-2552-1
HARDCOVER ISBN: 979-8-3852-2553-8
EBOOK ISBN: 979-8-3852-2554-5

VERSION NUMBER 10/16/25

Contents

Foreword

FOR THE GOSPEL OF MARK to declare that the kin-dom of God belongs to the children is disarming (Mark 10:13-16). It is disarming because we are invited to receive the kin-dom not with swords but with the vulnerability of playful children. Osvaldo Vena reminds us once again that the Gospel is counterintuitive and even subversive because we are invited to be and act like a child in order to receive the kin-dom of God.

To act like a child implies the possibility of being rebuked (Mark 10:13). As a parent of two young children, there are moments in which my children's playful spirit irritates other adults and even myself. Like the disciples, I also spoke sternly to them because dealing with tantrums is not for the fainthearted. I am reticent to bring my children to certain church functions due to the possibility of unforeseen disruptions. And yet, Jesus tells us that the children are not only welcome but that the kin-dom of God belongs to them. We are even encouraged to receive the kin-dom of God like a little child in order to enter it.

Here is where Vena reminds us that we also were once children. We also rejoiced in our unbounded and imaginative play. We immersed ourselves with the courage to explore. Vena brings us back to those moments of joy and courage with the uplifting poems written by the children of Palestine/Israel and Argentina. These poems resonate with many children around the world even today, particularly for children who are suffering under the oppressive structures created by the adults. These poems express both vulnerability and longing for a more vibrant future filled with peace, justice, and dignity for all children.

Vena's intertextual juxtaposition of the Gospel of Mark and children's poems is liberating because many of us overlook how our reading of the Bible is based on gerontocentrism,[1] or the preferential treatment of adulthood and adult perspective as normative. As Vena cautions, we have been reading *for* the children. We barely listen to them. Vena's cautionary and creative project invites us to read passages such as Mark 10:13-16 with childist hermeneutics.[2] This hermeneutics is not about being childish; far from it. Rather, childist hermeneutics unearths the voiceless and suppressed presence/absence of children in the Bible and in the current world. Vena does so with the poems of children from Palestine/Israel and Argentina. Their poetry helps us read the Gospel of Mark in creative and liberating ways.

I admire Vena's childist hermeneutics because he guides us in dismantling hegemonic narratives on maturity. Vena's work follows the enduring history of resistance led by feminists, womanists, postcolonialists, nonhuman activists, and other activist voices. Vena reminds us that the concept of childhood is a social and cultural construct.[3] In other words, childhood is defined by arbitrary structures and symbolisms that impose markers or stages of maturity. After all, some of us feel like we have never matured or live up to the so-called standards of adulthood. Meanwhile, some children are more mature than adults, either by their choosing or because they were forced to be so. In all of these, we are invited to listen to children as they read the Bible, as they write their poems about the world, and as they tell us better futures to come.

Moreover, children show us the value of play. Neoliberalism or the market-driven efficiency model in which individuals are measured by their productivity has incarcerated our adult souls. We forgot the value of play because we constantly measure ourselves and each other with profit and productivity. Children

1. Jenks, *Childhood*; Ellis, "'God Was with the Child.'"
2. Wall, "Childhood Studies."
3. James and Prout, *Constructing and Reconstructing Childhood*.

remind us that there is another way of being and becoming that liberates our souls from the oppressive productivity-based value systems. Playing liberates the soul and even the body to realms of possibilities, to spaces of joy and unfettered relationality with myself and the other. Playing has joy as its end; and it is okay to be simply happy. In particular, children who are in war-torn areas need to play; they deserve to be happy. The children of Gaza, Israel, Argentina, Democratic Republic of the Congo, North Korea, and other places need to play in the playground of joy.

We, the interpreters of the Bible, need to play too. That is, we cannot continue locking ourselves in the stale room of historicity. With poems and stories, Vena shows us a way in which we could also be in the playground of the joyous, creative, deconstructive, and liberating reading of the Bible. We are also invited to listen to the prophetic and piercing words of children who recognize oppression but do not dwell in its misery. As they find artistic hope under the rubble of poverty and homelessness, we are also invited to find hope amid vulnerability. After all, we are all children of God.

Will you join us as we play together in the playground of God?

Dong Hyeon Jeong
Garrett-Evangelical Theological Seminary

Acknowledgments

I WANT TO ACKNOWLEDGE the influence of many people on the writing of this book. First up, Dr. K. K. Yeo and Dr. Melanie Baffes, who originally invited me to write it and gave me valuable insight into its production. Unfortunately, the series they were coediting was interrupted, and I had to find a new publisher, which turned out to be Wipf and Stock.

Second, Sophia Twaddell, who has edited several of my books. Her insights have been crucial in improving my writing to the point that I couldn't imagine embarking on another project without her help.

Third, Dr. Dong Hyeon Jeong, my colleague at Garrett-Evangelical Theological Seminary, who joined the institution during my last year of teaching. He and I shared many things in common, among them our love for the Gospel of Mark and hermeneutics. Another was the influence of missionaries in our lives, he as a MK (missionary kid) and I as one deeply marked by their teaching. Also, both have been racially minoritized in this country, which makes us deeply aware of how people look at us.

Finally, I have to mention the children's poets from Palestine, Israel, and Argentina. Without their poems this book wouldn't have existed in the form it does. They gave me the inspiration to do something new, something I have not seen yet—that is, using poetry as hermeneutical key into the biblical text.

As always, I recognize the support of my family, my wife, sons, and grandchildren, an ever-present reality behind every word I write.

To all of them goes my gratitude.

Osvaldo D. Vena
March of 2025

Introduction

IN THIS BOOK I want to bring into dialogue two communities. One is the hypothetical community of Mark, which can be reconstructed behind the Gospel. It is a community that is locked in place and time: the first century Mediterranean world. It is made up of adults and children in a hierarchical relationship that places the former over the latter, speaking for them rather than allowing them to speak for themselves. Nevertheless, this community has left us with a text that, because of its very nature as a text, is not locked into its original meaning but is open to new and numerous interpretations produced by a variety of interpretive communities.

The other is a contemporary, real community whose members are children living in Israel/Palestine and in Argentina. This community has also produced a text—in this case poetry—which is also open to new and numerous interpretations. I have termed this "the community of the playground."

Each community will contribute with its own literary production. Mark will bring his narrative, his prose; the children, their poetry. Therefore, it is going to be an intertextual exercise that uses two different types of text.

The term "intertextuality" was first developed by Julia Kristeva in 1969. It describes every discourse, written or spoken, which in her view is intertextual, "a field of transpositions of various signifying systems,"[1] "an intersection of textual surfaces rather than a

---

1. Kristeva, *Revolution*, 60.

1

point (a fixed meaning)."[2] Every text then is an intersection of texts that are themselves intersections, overlaps, and collisions of other texts. To use her words, every text is a "mosaic of quotations," an intertext without center or boundaries.[3] The Gospel of Mark is a text included in a canon of sacred literature, but it is also a text in the broader sense of the term, and it is in this manner that I want to approach it and bring it into dialogue with the text of the children's poetry, keeping in mind Kristeva's definition of texts. One can expect that because texts have no center or boundaries, the dialogue between the Gospel and the children's poems will be free and fluid and capable of rending unexpected meanings and relationships, but that needs to be proven.

In my understanding of children, I am following Rubem Alves's definition of what a child's very nature is. What is a child? asks Alves. What is it that characterizes a child? It is play. And what is play? It is nonproductive activity. It does not produce objects, but it delivers pleasure, joy, which is an end in itself. He reminds us of Freud's concept that the more primordial drive in life is the pleasure principle.[4] The children whose poems I am highlighting in this book have not become adults yet, so their poetry is part of this play. They respond to their reality not as grown-ups but as children, before they are forced to become adults against their own desires, through a process of socialization and education, "programs whereby we impose our reality on the weak—namely children—through a subtle brainwashing process or a not-so-subtle exercise of physical and psychological coercion."[5] These are not poems written by adults, experts in literature, but by playful children. Paraphrasing something Pablo Picasso once said, "Every child is an artist. The problem is how to remain an artist once he grows up."

My specific focus for this book will be the appeal to and deployment of an early Christian text, the Gospel of Mark, and its

2. Kristeva, *Desire in Language*, 65.

3. Kristeva, *Desire in Language*, 66.

4. Alves, *Tomorrow's Child*, 86–87.

5. Alves, *Tomorrow's Child*, 85.

assumed context in first-century Palestine during the time of the First Jewish-Roman War (66–71 CE) by means of a cultural-artistic tool—namely, the poetry of Palestinian, Jewish, and Argentine children. This poetry will serve as a catalyst of two global systemic manifestations of violence against children: one, war and occupation; the other, marginalization and homelessness. The poems will provide the children's personal experience of these manifestations. The Gospel of Mark will provide a road map for how imperial and wartime violence may have affected the children of the Markan community.

The Gospel of Mark is a text written by an unknown first century male, reflecting his understanding of the place and plight of children in first-century Roman-occupied Palestine in general and in his community in particular. He speaks "for" children. He "represents" them as they had no voice of their own at the time the Gospel of Mark was written. On the other hand, the poems of the children living in Israel and the occupied territories of Palestine today reflect their own take on reality, as does the poetry of the Argentine children. No one represents them. They speak for themselves. The Palestinian/Israeli children tell us about how war affects them, and the Argentine children contend, among other things, with the issue of extreme poverty and its concomitant consequences of homelessness and exploitation. Without getting too political, the Palestinian children are also dealing with poverty and homelessness as a result of the occupation of the West Bank and Gaza as Israel continues to try to bomb Hamas out of existence. Both the Gospel and the children's poems are visionary and eschatological texts, for they do not describe reality objectively but subjectively—that is, filtered through their own perspectives—thus prescribing a course of action that we are invited to follow.[6]

---

6. Here I would like to affirm Sallie McFague's concept of *atopia* rather than *utopia*. She distinguishes between the two by saying that while *utopia* refers to an ideal community to which we can point where the new vision is being realized, *atopia* points at an imagined world both prophetic and alluring from which we can judge what is wrong with the present paradigm. I suggest that this is precisely what the children's poems do. *Body of God*, 198.

In this book, I will try—as much as I can—not to speak for children but to have them speak for themselves. I will do that by highlighting in their poems themes, desires, and dreams that will allow us to see the world through their eyes rather than through our own. I am hoping that this will enable us, as global scholars, to situate our research in an appropriate and realistic context.[7] But I will also try to find those themes in Mark and see how they relate to the children's themes. If what Kristeva affirms about texts is correct—that is, that they are intersections, overlaps, and collisions of other texts—then by finding common themes we should be able to bring them into a meaningful dialogue.

The poems I will be analyzing were written by children living in Israel/Palestine during the tumultuous times of the 1970s and by children living in Argentina during the process of democratization that, starting in 1983, followed the overthrow of the military regime that had plunged the country into chaos and corruption.[8] These poems are their way of coping with their oppression; therefore, they can be used as catalysts for the systemic violence exercised against them and as cultural[9] points of entry into the biblical text. And they come not only from the culture of children in general but also from regional manifestations of that culture.

Why is poetry so important? What does it convey that prose does not? What aspects of reality does it tap into that prose does not? For one thing, poetry is an open universe. Prose is a closed one; it is a path readers are prompted to follow guided by the narrative strategy of the writer. Prose is linear whereas poetry is circular, and

7. See here Borg and Crossan, *First Paul*; and Mills, *Racial Contract*.

8. The poems written by Palestinian and Jewish children come from the book *My Shalom My Peace: Paintings and Poems by Jewish and Arab Children*, edited and designed by Jacob Zim and first published in 1974 under the title *Hashalom Sheli* by American Israel Publishing and Sonol, Israel. The English translation was published in 1975 by Sabra Books and distributed in the US by McGraw-Hill. The poem excerpts have been reproduced here with permission from McGraw-Hill. The poems in Spanish are not published and come from children living in the Hidden City (Ciudad Oculta) in Buenos Aires; they are reproduced here with permission from the authors.

9. Many authors acknowledge that children have their specific culture. See for example, Jenkins, *Children's Culture Reader*.

it deconstructs the power of the narrator. Poetry does two things: it interprets the present and envisions the future in ways that are totally unrelated to the present. That is why it is a utopia. Prose, on the other hand, is pragmatic; it does not interpret the present but defines it and sees the future as a continuation of the present. It is closed, concrete, and limited while poetry is open, imaginative, and unlimited. Prose becomes repetitive; poetry does not.

Prose and poetry are literary first cousins, with poetry often being recognized as the matrix of prose,[10] but while the language of prose is straightforward, the language of poetry may not be. Prose uses ordinary, everyday language to create a narrative, but poetry often uses figurative and symbolic language along with rhythm, rhyme, and line breaks to convey meaning through metaphor, sarcasm, irony, and euphemism, among other things.[11] Reading prose, the rhetorical construction of the author is the road the reader has to take in order to understand what the author meant to say with the story. Prose is guided interpretation, whereas poetry, on the other hand, tells a story that is hidden between the interstices of its cadence, rhyme, and meter. Its meaning is not necessarily clear at all. It is open to interpretation, speculation, misunderstanding, imagination, creative thinking, fantasy, and so on. Poetry is free, while prose is limited, conditioned by the story it is telling. But both have something in common: language. And it is there where we hope that the intertextual dialogue between Mark's narrative and the children' poems will take place.

What do we hope to obtain in the process? On the one hand, more insight into the Gospel of Mark, a new way to decipher its meaning potential by using the children's poems as an interpretive tool. On the other, to unravel the intricate web of the poems by

10. Franke, "Poetry." For a complete list of his work, consult Wikipedia, "William Franke."

11. "Poetry is language marked as different from ordinary speech. The strange effects of sound in poetic language seem to have a sense that is not that of everyday speech and rather makes sense in another way than that to which we are accustomed. Poetry is meaningful not by reference to the things that are before us in the sensible world but by evocations of things unseen or seen in their higher meanings." Franke, "Poetry."

bringing them in conversation with a text that expresses similar themes and concerns. The goal is a rereading of both texts that will render them relevant for new audiences in such a way that a person who reads the gospel but is unaware of the existence of these poems will miss out on the intertextuality that they provide. The same can be said of any reader of the poems alone. Because I realize that regardless of any efforts in the past to interpret the gospel using poems as a tool, this specific combination has never been tried, at least not that I am aware of.

Let us embark then in this hermeneutical journey of which we only know the beginning but not the end.

Chapter 1

Children as Cultural and Theological Constructs

CHILDREN IN THE BIBLE

In Gen 1–2, God creates humans as adults, as models of/for humanity. That seems to suggest that for the biblical writer of that text, full humanity exists only in adults. Nevertheless, in some of the Old Testament narratives concerning leaders of the people such as Samuel, Isaac, Joseph, etc., children acquire some relevance. Likewise, in the New Testament, Jesus' birth is given prominence, at least in Matthew and Luke. And the apocryphal Gospels, such as the Protoevangelium of James and the Infancy Gospel of Thomas, show a keen interest in Jesus as a child.

In the Gospels, Jesus makes children models/examples for the new community he is envisioning. When in Luke 6:20 Jesus, looking at his disciples, says, "Blessed are you who are poor, for yours is the kingdom of God,"[1] he seems to be equating them with children, who were the poorest of the poor, and may have been thinking of them as models for his followers. If the poor stand here for children, what does it mean that the kingdom of God *belongs* to children? Is it a poetic way of saying that "they get it" whereas

---

1. Throughout this book I will be using the New International Version (NIV) for the New Testament texts and the New Revised Standard Version (NRSV) for those in the Hebrew Bible.

adults don't? Is it a way of criticizing power as embodied in the people and institutions of the Greco-Roman world, the wider context for the writing of the Gospels? If that is the case then Jesus, as a *character* of the story being told, is used as a means of such criticism, regardless of what the Jesus of history may have thought about children in general and children in relation to the forthcoming kingdom of God. At any rate, the portrayal of children in both the Old Testament and the New Testament are cultural constructs that say little about the real authors' understanding.

CHILDREN AS CULTURAL CONSTRUCTS

There is no universal idea of what a child is, nor is there a specific location in time and space that could be seen as normative for the definition of children.[2] In Mark, the author, guided by his cultural understanding of childhood,[3] inscribes in the text his own subjective reading of these cultural norms in such a way that his treatment of children may be different from another author in the same time and place. Every reading is subjective, and Mark is not an exception.

In the wider Hellenistic society, children were marginalized, especially female children. They were not regarded as legal persons

2. The bibliography on this subject is extensive. Here are just a few examples: Archard, *Children*; Cohen, *Jewish Family in Antiquity*; Cooper, *Child in Jewish History*; Grassi, *Children's Liberation*; Nathan, *Family in Late Antiquity*; Somerville, *Rise and Fall of Childhood*; Flynn, *Children in the Bible*.

3. In today's world childhood is generally defined as ages one through twelve/thirteen, and it ends when the person reaches puberty. But in the ancient world life spans were much shorter. Childhood was not defined as a distinct, protected period of life as it is today; rather, children were largely viewed as small adults, expected to contribute to the family workforce at a young age. Children seven years of age and under were considered infants and were under the care of women. From age eight until they reached adulthood, children were expected to help with housework. The age of adulthood was twelve for girls and fourteen for boys. It is this understanding of childhood that I assume Mark had when he wrote his Gospel. Regents of the University of Michigan, "Archaeologies of Childhood."

and, like women, were not counted in crowds.[4] According to Bruce Malina, "Children were the weakest, most vulnerable members of society. Infant mortality rates sometimes reached 30 percent. Another 30 percent of live births were dead by age six, and 60 percent were gone by age sixteen."[5]

In the Jewish community at least, the male child was given a status as a member of the covenant through circumcision. But such right was not given to the female child, who could only belong to the covenant community indirectly through her father, and later through her husband.[6] Even though there were exceptions in the Greco-Roman world that show that children were appreciated and taken care of, as shown in sarcophagi that depict the child's favorite pastime,[7] they did not have an intrinsic value as children but a functional one as guarantors of the family's status. They were considered "vital in large agrarian societies such as Greece and Rome for their role as heir of the family state and property."[8]

In an unpublished essay, Jeffrey Koetje deals with what he calls the problem of childhood. He says,

> Childhood is a concept and although childhood is played out in real children's lives, it has as much, if not more, to do with adult ideologies and adult idealisms as it does with flesh-and-blood youngsters. As an ideological concept, it is socio-culturally constructed, which means that there have been and are as many ideas and ideals about what children should be, how they should act, what they are capable or incapable of doing as there have been and are societies into which children are born and raised.[9]

What interests us in this work is the social-cultural construction of childhood in the first-century Greco-Roman world, where the Gospel of Mark was written. In this world, there were two

4. In Mark 6:44, Jesus feeds five thousand men (*andres*).

5. Malina and Rohrbaugh, *Social Science Commentary*, 11.

6. Okure, "Children in Mark," 130.

7. "Childs sarcophagus Stock Photos and Images."

8. Murphy, *Kids and Kingdom*, 52.

9. Koetje, "We're His Damn Kids," 2.

beliefs held in tension: children were not-yet-human, and at the same time childhood was seen as a stage of life and not simply a preparation for adult life. The drastic ideological and physical separation made between childhood and adulthood in modern Western societies was far less than in ancient ones. One example of this is the use of children's labor alongside the toiling of adults.[10]

If childhood at the time of Mark's writing is an ideological concept and as such can only be known through texts,[11] how do we know how much of that construction reflects real children's lives and how much reflects the author's perception of it? There usually is a great degree of separation between what is ideally conceptualized and what is actually played out in real life.[12] According to Koetje, this is aggravated by the fact that there are few surviving records of what children were actually like. We might have a good sense of how a society may have constructed the ideal childhood, but that does not mean that we have a good understanding, if any at all, of how children *actually* experienced childhood. It is "the difficulty—if not outright impossibility—of 'translating' ideology and idealism in the conceptualization of childhood into the realities of historical children."[13]

Koetje wrote his essay in 2003. Since then, much research has been done on the subject of childhood in the ancient world, with the result that the opinion of scholars has changed. Now we have a pretty good idea about children's lives in the ancient world. One important insight of this updated scholarship is that in the ancient world, children were valued and vulnerable.[14] Like today, parents were sleep-deprived by the sleepless child, so lullabies had to be used in order to calm them down. There is an example of such a song in an ancient Babylonian text, written between 1894 and 1595 BCE, where the "sleep-deprived mother begs the child to

10. Koetje, "We're His Damn Kids," 2.
11. For we only know reality through texts.
12. Koetje, "We're His Damn Kids" 3.
13. Koetje, "We're His Damn Kids," 3.
14. These ideas are taken from Flynn and Garroway, "Children."

fall asleep like one passed out drunk."[15] But the night brought also danger with it. When a child would suddenly die in her sleep, what is known today as sudden infant death syndrome, it was attributed to the demoness Lilith or Lamashtu, two distinct figures, who would come at night and breastfeed the baby with poisonous milk. In order to ward off this demoness, parents would place amulets around the child and leave a lamp burning so as to scare away "bad things" that may occur.

But children also moved in and out of domestic units through adoption and slavery, which shows how contradictory society's attitude toward children has often been. These two social institutions have been well documented in ancient documents. For example, a four-thousand-year-old poem from the ancient cities of Nuzi, Emar, and Nippur encourages parents to adopt children with deformities, thus finding a place for them in society.

The ancient Babylonian Code of Hammurabi, specifically laws 185–195, shows that formal adoptions came with a strict set of rules so the child could be fully integrated into the new family. But this was not always desired. Sometimes parents withdrew legal responsibility for a child. One set of texts discusses this in terms of children being "thrown to the dog's mouth," a reference to the local dump where children could be left, a sort of "safe-drop" zone. These children often entered a life of slavery. Ultimately, coming to a greater understanding of children in history raises important questions for how societies respond or not to children's vulnerability. The challenge of protecting the most vulnerable has not disappeared.[16]

Now, we could say that vulnerability has positive and negative connotations. There is a vulnerability that is assumed by *choice* by those who have power and who give it up temporarily in order to accomplish an objective. This can be seen in many fields of study. In psychology, for instance, we see it in the patient who shows a voluntary vulnerability when agreeing to the treatment of the psychiatrist. In sociology, we see it when a king allows himself

15. Flynn and Garroway, "Children."
16. Flynn and Garroway, "Children."

to be ridiculed by mimes and jesters in order to release pressure from people's discontent so he can continue to oppress them. And in theology, it is expressed as *kenosis*, the emptying of a given condition in order to benefit others, the supreme example of which is Jesus when he not only became a human but a slave, the lowest position of the society of the time, lower even than that of children and women. This idea is reflected in the hymn used (or composed) by Paul in Phil 2:7–11 when he says that Jesus, even though he was in the form of God, did not consider this a privilege to hang on to but took on human form and became a slave. Even though ontologically (being) he was God, functionally (doing) he was like a slave, thus providing a model to be imitated by the believers.

Another biblical passage that builds on the concept of vulnerability is Mark 10:13–16, where Jesus admonishes his disciples to become like children if they wish to ever enter into the kingdom. But first the kingdom has to be received as a little child would receive a gift—that is, being unable to reciprocate it in kind, as adults were supposed to do, lest they should be dishonored. Then, and only then, can the kingdom be enjoyed. One accesses the kingdom through vulnerability, not through power and privilege. Children's condition is thus spiritualized and made into an example to be imitated.

This kind of vulnerability is not what we talk about when we say that children are vulnerable, for in their case it refers to a *condition*, not to a choice—this condition being the absence of power. This happens to children in general, whether in the first or in the twenty-first century, though its degree varies according to their social location. Children who are well cared for by their parents may experience little or no vulnerability. In fact, they may experience the opposite: privilege. Privilege can confer the sort of security that may exclude physical, psychological, or emotional vulnerability. But at the same time, a child can be surrounded by privilege and still be exploited by adults in all of the aspects listed above.

The children who wrote the poems we shall study are vulnerable, and because of that they are subject to abuse. The only power they have is the visionary power of prophecy conveyed by their poetry, through which they challenge the world of the adults. They speak truth to power, and so they become God's voice to an unjust world.

Texts—especially religious ones—that talk about childhood are prescriptive, not descriptive. It is one thing to say what children ought to be like, or to do, and quite another to say what they actually were like, or did. In other words, they are ideal constructions that reflect the ideology of the authors, who most of the time are not reporting facts but trying to influence their readers so they may accept their point of view. Therefore, it would be very pertinent for this work to know how Mark constructs children. In other words, what is it about children that he wants his readers to accept?

CHILDREN AS THEOLOGICAL CONSTRUCTS

No one would seriously deny that Mark is trying to convince his audience that Jesus is the Messiah and the Son of God who has taken the role of the Son of Man of the intertestamental literature in a new way. This is pretty clear. But what about other themes, such as the role of the male disciples and of women and children in his community? How are these characters dealt with in the story? Historically? Rhetorically? Both? We are particularly interested in Mark's portrayal of children not only in his community but in the broader Palestinian society.

Mark mentions children in Mark 7:27, 28; 9:36; 10:13–15, 24, 29–30; 12:19–22; and 13:12. In these places, he uses the technical terms *teknon* and *paeidion*. He also refers to them without using a technical term, as in 5:21–24a, 35–43, and 9:14–29, where he uses *thugatrion* (little daughter) and *korasion* (girl). Some of these instances refer to his community and some to the broader Palestinian society. Let's examine them.

THE GOSPEL AND THE PLAYGROUND

Mark 5:21–24a, 35–43; 9:14–29

Jairus's daughter, whom Jesus heals even though everyone thought she was dead, was twelve years old. The boy possessed by an impure spirit, whom Jesus healed, was in that condition from childhood (*paidiothen*). These two examples, plus that of the daughter of the Syrophoenician woman of 7:27–28, prompts Ched Myers to ask, "For where do we meet children in the Gospel? In every case, it is in a situation of sickness or oppression."[17] And he will conclude by saying that Mark understands the child as victim.

Mark 7:27, 28

Children here stand for the people of Israel as opposed to the gentiles, who are represented by the Syrophoenician woman. Clues from the culture of the time suggest that real children were being fed in a nurturing context, a house, but this time something interfered. The woman's daughter was possessed by a demon, and she asked Jesus to cast it out. He refuses but she insists, alleging that even the dogs eat from the crumbs falling from the table. Embarrassed, Jesus complies, and the little girl is liberated. Two things stand out about how children were treated: they were fed, and when sick, a means of healing was provided, in this case by Jesus who played the role of a wandering exorcist. Even though boys were usually given special attention, it is remarkable that here it is a girl who receives the care she needs.

Mark 9:36–37

Jesus makes here an incredible claim. The disciples were discussing, on the way, who in the group would have the greatest honor, but they were embarrassed to tell Jesus, so they kept quiet. But Jesus knew his disciples and figured it out. He reverses society's mores and tells them that if they want to be first, they have to be

---

17. Myers, *Binding the Strong Man*, 268.

willing to be last. Then he teaches them an object lesson. He takes a little child (*paidion*) in his arms and uses it as an example. To be last means to be like a child, who was certainly last in the social ranking of the times. He is not talking about the innocence of the child but about his vulnerability. And he goes on to say, "Whoever welcomes one such child in my name welcomes me" (Mark 9:37a). Jesus was present in the most powerless group of the times. Welcoming children—that is, extending hospitality to them—meant extending hospitality to Jesus, the suffering and crucified one. In turn, it amounted to welcoming the one who sent Jesus, the God of Israel: "And whoever welcomes me welcomes not me but the one who sent me" (Mark 9:37b).

Morna Hooker suggests that this passage reflects the Jewish belief that a person's agent or representative should be received as the person themselves, and backs it up with Matt 10:40–42 and Luke 10:16.[18] This idea is developed by Matthew in the parable of the sheep and the goats (Matt 25:31–46). Therefore, to put a stumbling block[19] before them is a recipe for damnation, as seen in Mark 9:42–50, a section that follows naturally from 9:33–37 but which has been interrupted by the reference to the exorcist of 9:38–41. Later in this work we will propose an interpretation for these verses as a possible reference to pederasty.

Mark 10:13–16

People were bringing little children (*paidia*) to Jesus so he might bless them. These people were obviously parents who wanted to protect their children from the vicissitudes of life, such as sicknesses and evil spirits. They believed that a blessing from a holy man would protect them. The blessing was performed by physical contact.[20] First, he took them in his arms, then he placed his hands

18. Hooker, *Mark*, 28.

19. The word for stumbling block is *skandalizo*. It could be translated "to scandalize," which means "to offend by some improper or unconventional conduct," "to shock," "to reproach," or "to disgrace." Vena, "Blessing," 146.

20. See Gen 48:14 where blessing is being conveyed by touching. In Mark,

on them and blessed them. This action of Jesus speaks of children's need of protection, which can most vividly be experienced by human contact. We do not know the age or gender of these children; they were probably very young boys and girls, but also, based on the fact that in 5:39 the word *paidion* is used for a twelve-year-old girl, some of them could have been close to the time when children were entering adulthood.

The disciples reacted harshly to Jesus' action and rebuked those who were bringing the children. This may have been due to their own understanding of the relationship between children and adults. Children were not supposed to interfere in the grown-up world and especially when the adult in question was a teacher. In their minds, Jesus' message of the kingdom was for adults, not for children. But Jesus says exactly the opposite: it is first and utmost for children,[21] and adults benefit from it as long as they have the same attitude toward it as children do (more about this below).

touching Jesus is always done in order to convey some benefit (e.g., the leper in Mark 1:41, the crowd by the seaside in 3:10, the hemorrhaging woman in 5:27–28; see also 6:56, 8:22). Blessing a person (verse 16) is also a way of conveying a benefit. Attridge, *Harper Collins Study Bibile*, 1743.

21. Mark 10:14. This passage suggests that children, for their very nature, are already in the kingdom. Their vulnerability gives them the privilege of enjoying the kingdom as a present reality. The following poem from the Tao Te Ching (Lao Tzu, *Tao Te Ching* 76) says it in a different way:

Men are born soft and supple;
dead, they are stiff and hard.
Plants are born tender and pliant;
dead, they are brittle and dry.

Thus whoever is stiff and inflexible
is a disciple of death.
Whoever is soft and yielding
is a disciple of life.

The hard and stiff will be broken.
The soft and supple will prevail.

"Stiff" and "inflexible" define an adult, "soft" and "yielding" a child. The former will be broken, says Tao Ching, the latter will prevail.

If we limit ourselves to the Gospel of Mark as a literary work, we could say that the reason for the disciples' reaction is that in 9:33–37, Jesus had already told them that children were models of the kind of attitude needed among their group, an attitude of service to all. Here, in typical Markan fashion, the disciples still don't get it. No wonder Jesus is angry!

Mark 10:24, 29, 30

In these verses the word for children is *tekna*. It refers figuratively to the disciples (verse 24) and to actual, real children (verses 29, 30). When speaking of the disciples as children, we should not see it as demeaning but as a term of endearment, as a father would speak to his children. In a similar manner, the author of 1 John refers to his congregation with the same word, *teknia*, in 1 John 2:1, 12, 28; 3:7; 4:4; and 5:21 (but uses *paidia* in 2:14 and 18). The context, both in Mark and in 1 John, is one of teaching. A father figure is dispensing knowledge that the children are absorbing. The children of verses 29 and 30 are real and part of the household. They share it with brothers, sisters, mother, and father. But the unsettling thought is that because of the disciples following Jesus, they have been left uncared-for. One can only wonder about what really happened to these children and who took care of them when left alone. The promise of receiving a hundred times more in this present age, which includes children, may try to compensate for this apparent lack of concern by incorporating them into a new, alternative community where their needs are met. This community is the Jesus movement, which Mark—removed from the Jesus of history by nearly forty years, and based on the oral traditions he received—is constructing for his audience. But still the doubt persists as to the fate of the children of the Markan community.

As A. James Murray puts it, "Are they [children] celebrated or exploited, protected or abandoned by adult characters in the Synoptic accounts?"[22]

22. Murphy, *Kids and Kingdom*, 35.

Mark 12:19, 20–22

Here Mark uses the word *teknon* for children but also the word *sperma*, meaning "male children" in this context but "descendants" in a broader sense. Male children were the key to the continuity and success of the patriarchal system, which was passed from fathers to sons. Having male children was an asset because it guaranteed social status and honor.[23] Therefore, the law provided the levirate marriage, whereby the brother of a man who died without descendants was to marry the widow and raise up offspring for his brother (Deut 25:5–6). In the Sadducees' view, children are not considered for their own worth but only as a means to an end: continuation of the patriarchal system. They have value not in themselves but as a commodity, something needed to consolidate and perpetuate the family. That is why they produced the hypothetical case of a woman who was married to seven brothers. They wanted to know whose wife she would be at the resurrection, a loaded and hypocritical question since they did not believe in the resurrection.

Mark has a different opinion, so he has Jesus saying that when the dead rise they will neither marry nor be given in marriage but will be like the angels in heaven, thus overruling patriarchy in favor of a more egalitarian system that will happen at the resurrection of the dead. We have an anticipation of this in Mark 10:29–30 when, listing the members of the alternative family he is proposing, he fails to mention fathers, the head of the patriarchal family. It is almost as a case study for life after the resurrection!

Mark 13:12

The enmity between parents and children mentioned by Mark in 13:12 is a traditional apocalyptic motif (see Mic 7:6; 2 Esd 6:24),[24]

---

23. There were some exceptions. See for example Num 27:5–11.

24. The disintegration of family life due to a lack of trust among its members informs Micah's oracle. He describes family life under the threat of the Assyrian invasion, painting a gloomy picture of betrayal, distrust, and plain

but it probably happened among first-century believers especially during the time of the Jewish-Roman war. It is not impossible that children were used as informants by the authorities in order to break the family's allegiance to the movement.[25] Judas seems to have played that role in the Gospel narrative (Mark 3:19; 14:10, 43–46).

Summary

A quick summary of the preceding analysis renders the following conclusions:

1. Children were nurtured and protected in the household by caring parents, but that did not preclude them from being victims of sickness and oppression, realities that transcend the home.

2. Children are used as examples of those who have the greatest honor because they are the least and the last in the social ranking. At the same time, because of their vulnerability, they have to be protected from sexual abuse by adults.

3. Children receive the protection and blessing of Jesus, who sees them as already embodying *the* kingdom.

4. Sometimes children are left uncared-for when their parents join the Jesus movement, but this is balanced off when Jesus promises his followers an alternative family.

5. Children are seen by the Sadducees as commodities, as means for perpetuating the patriarchal family. Mark, though, sees them as having intrinsic value.

---

enmity, as people take sides in the approaching and inevitable fate of the nation.

25. For a description of the ancient and modern-day role of informants, including that of children, see Rich, "Use of Citizen Informants." See also Tamez, "Conflict in Mark," 108–9, where she talks about the role of the informant in the Colombian guerrilla war, something known as *sapeo*, "frogging," and which entails "the betrayal of someone for profit, or the act of being a longtime paid informant, obtaining information from any side."

6. Some children in his community may have been ideologically and emotionally exploited by the Romans as informants in order to destroy the Israelite family unity.

Mark is adamant as to the position of children in society and in his community. They are to be given a special position for being children; they are to be protected and cared for. He knows that often children are victimized by adults who take advantage of their vulnerability. For example, the Sadducees see them as patrimony, as a means to perpetuate the power of the patriarchal society. Herodias sees her daughter as a way to get her wishes of killing John the Baptist (Mark 6). The Romans see them as means to perpetuate their political power and use them as informants.

Mark is also clear as to what is—or should be—children's position in his community. That is why he puts them at the center of the community's life—as an example of how a disciple should behave. But he hints to the fact that even in the community, they can be subjected to abuse, perhaps even sexual abuse, which deserves the evangelist's harshest condemnation in the entire Gospel. It is only in Mark 9:42–50 that Mark uses the word for hell (*gehenna*) and does so possibly in connection with pederasty. It seems as if in Mark, the ones who end up in hell are those who abuse children and not necessarily those who disagree with Jesus' message, as the mention of the wandering exorcist of 9:38–41 seems to suggest.

There are at least four different opinions among scholars about the place and role of children in the Markan community, some of which agree with our findings above:

1. *Children are cared for and protected and the center of the community's life.* There is general consensus among scholars that Mark 9:36–37 is a reference to actual children. What is not so clear is if Mark 9:42 refers also to children or if it is a way of talking about believers. But if it refers to actual children, then the three warnings to those who scandalize them (verses 43–48) can be interpreted as a warning against pederasty.[26] Thus the evangelist seems to go against the prevailing mode

26. Loader, *Sexuality and the Jesus Tradition*, 23.

in the Greco-Roman society to use children as source of pleasure. In his community, adult males will behave differently.

2. *Children are abandoned by adults when they joined the Jesus movement.* In his book *Kids and Kingdom*, A. James Murphy concludes that even though many have interpreted the passages in Mark that refer to children as the evangelist's way to challenge the marginalization of children by making them the center of the community life through the example of Jesus who embraced them and brought them to close proximity with him, still the overall message of this Gospel is that while the narrative continues "children appear less; Jesus and the disciples move on."[27]

3. *Children are used as examples for adult disciples.* Many scholars conclude that this is the primary use of children in Mark: as foils for the adults' discipleship.[28] If that is the case, then their mention is only for the sake of the adults of the community. Children are objectifications of the kingdom, visual reminders and examples of what it is to be in the kingdom.

4. *Children are appreciated for their intrinsic value.* Teresa Okure has given substantial evidence that in Mark children have an intrinsic value as children. She says that they should be seen "not just as foils for proclaiming the kingdom but as people who in their own right are presented by the Jesus of the Gospels as having a place in the kingdom as children."[29]

While disagreeing with Murphy, Hooker, and Witherington, who see children as models for adult's discipleship, I agree with Okure in suggesting that the Markan community, informed and influenced by a still fresh memory of the Jesus of history, appreciated children for their intrinsic value. Regrettably, some people in the community were actually abusing them, imitating the sexual exploitation of children in the Greco-Roman world. Newcomers,

27. Murphy, *Kids and Kingdom*, 102.

28. See here Hooker, *Mark*, 238–39; Witherington, *Gospel of Mark*, 278–80.

29. Okure, "Children in Mark," 143.

especially, would bring their sexual mores and habits into the community; therefore, Mark felt the need to protect the children by invoking an aphorism spoken by Jesus in order to address a situation that had arisen, and which was threatening to undermine the life of the group.

CONCLUSION

In this chapter I have dealt with children as cultural and theological constructs. I have reached certain conclusions based on texts that prescribe the authors' ideas of what children are and/or do in order to influence their readers. Thus, these texts are ideological. Furthermore, my own reading of those texts is subjective, conditioned by my social location.

It is this interplay of subjectivities that renders objectivity impossible. The children of these texts are very different from the ones I see every day, so in order to make a connection between the two, I have to engage in a hermeneutical exercise. This piece represents such an exercise.

Chapter 2

Common Themes in Mark and the Poems

War and Extreme Poverty

THE VOICE OF THE EXPERTS is expressed in quantitative data, which by its very nature is hard and cold. In it, people are reduced to numbers. They are faceless, emotionless, and generic. This kind of data collection is typical of the epistemologies of the North which, pretending to be objective, rational, and scientific, advance only one valid form of knowing, something Segovia calls "epistemic exclusivism."[1]

The typical quantitative data concerning war and poverty as it relates to children will give us information about how many children were killed in past and present wars, how many became orphans, and how many were displaced, traumatized, used as soldiers, etc. Or it can indicate the number of children living in extreme poverty by city or by country and their use by adults as laborers, soldiers, and sex workers, all of this useful but cold data. In the age of the Internet, all this information is available to us immediately. But I am more interested in hearing the primary voices, the voices of the victims, expressed through qualitative data, which is more subjective, experiential, and biased by nature.

---

1. Segovia, "Criticism in Critical Times," 24.

WAR

The first theme I want to explore is war. War, a creation of patriarchy and the means by which the domination system is kept in place, turns humanity into a battlefield where only the violent and militarily powerful survive. Women, children, and minorities—sexual, racial, ethnic, and religious—are made the victims of the system's insatiable thirst for power. Children are the innocent casualties of war, expendable humans who happen to be in the wrong place at the wrong time—collateral damage. War interrupts children's childhood, making them into adults overnight. They are deprived of their human right to be children, to play, to dream. They are used in combat.[2] They are left orphans. They become refugees.[3] They lose their sense of belonging to a family and become easy prey of extremist groups, fictive families that take advantage of their predicament.[4]

Important as this information may be, it is the voice of the victims of war, the children themselves, that I am more interested in. And their voices speak of existential pain that cannot be placed on a chart, pain that can only be expressed through the arts, in this case poetry. When they do that, they are acting as contemporary prophets analogous to the ancient ones. I will discuss this further in the last chapter.

2. An estimated two hundred thousand to three hundred thousand children are used as soldiers throughout the world, information supplied by the Human Rights Watch official website, which also describes the use of children soldiers by country. Human Rights Watch, "Children Used as Soldiers."

3. An estimated 8.4 million children are affected by or among the refugees of the Syrian civil war (Sinha, "Children of Syria"). As we write these lines, we learn that "one month of war in Ukraine has led to the displacement of 4.3 million children—more than half of the country's estimated 7.5 million child population. This includes more than 1.8 million children who have crossed into neighbouring countries as refugees and 2.5 million who are now internally displaced inside Ukraine." UNICEF, "Ukraine's Children."

4. One of the latest, and more disturbing, aspects of how extremist groups are using children as soldiers is the case of Boko Haram in Nigeria. This group used forty-four children in suicide attacks in 2015, as opposed to four the year before. Three-quarters of them were girls. Jones, "Boko Haram."

The role of the prophets in Israel was serving as cultural critics and denouncers of social injustice, especially when it was perpetuated under the guise of piety and religious obeisance (Mic 6:6–8). Jeremiah and Micah, in the seventh and eighth centuries BCE respectively, are some of the best examples. Oftentimes, the way in which they conveyed their prophecies was through poetic oracles. This is true especially in the writings of Jeremiah, Micah, and Isaiah, to mention a few.

One can say that while prose reveals the prophet's dealings with the facts of present history, poetry reflects the prophet's interpretation of that history.[5] The prophet/poet takes the side of God even if that will bring him shame, persecution, and death (Jer 17:14–18, 20:7–18). He becomes intimate with God to the point of arguing with God and questioning God's motivations (Jer 12:1–4, 20:14–18). In the end, the prophet submits to the divine will but not before making his protest known. Jeremiah's poems are a skillful literary portrayal of this relationship as well as his final realization of God's absolute control over people's lives.

The children poets from Israel/Palestine demonstrate a similar relationship and realization. Their relationship with God is intimate and confident, as exemplified in the following excerpt from the poem "Prayer," written by a thirteen-year-old girl:

> And You, You won't deny the single wish of a girl.
> You created the Land of Peace,
> Where stands the City of Peace,
> Where stood the Temple of Peace,
> But where still there is no Peace . . .[6]

We find a similar daring intimacy with God in the poem "When Peace Will Finally Come," written also by a thirteen-year-old:

---

5. "Prophecy, in a central strand of Western literary tradition (coinciding to a degree with epic tradition), is not primarily about predicting the future. It is rather about seeing deeply into the overall meaning of history and the cosmos so as to be able to convey their truth in a way that is total and as such tantamount to a type of 'divine' revelation." Franke, "Poetry."

6. Shlomit Gossberg, "Prayer," in Zim, *My Shalom*, 6.

When the dove will find an olive branch
among the ocean's waves,
And when once more Your promise
You will keep
Perhaps—then—O Lord,
Peace will finally come?[7]

Notice the realism and honesty found in the words: "When once more Your promise / You will keep," which seems to suggest that at the present time God is not doing that! Also, the child poet is not sure that this will happen, so he/she confronts God with an open question: "Perhaps—then—O Lord, / Peace will finally come?" This questioning of God as the one who, in this child's view, could make peace happen is in tune with the best prophetic traditions of Israel that explore the issue of theodicy.

The poems address also the moral aspect of war. What is war to a child who has experienced it firsthand rather than through movies or video games? It is a terrifying nightmare. But more than that, it is a sin. The poem "A Bit of Peace," written by Moshe Cohen, age eleven, says it well:

If peace and war will ever meet
the peace will always win,
for peace is like a blessing
and war is like a sin.[8]

What would be the political ramifications of such a concept in a society that has justified war in the name of democracy and the free world? What would be the task of biblical scholars in elucidating the implications of such a view for our own Christian tradition of just war and redemptive violence? If this understanding of war as sinful is true—and I believe it is—then how can we as Christians in general, and biblical scholars in particular, address it? How can we avoid speaking to each other through countless rational arguments that do little to change the situation of children in the world? That, for me, is the real task, the task of the contemporary

---

7. Revital Ezrahi, "When Peace Will Finally Come," in Zim, *My Shalom*, 15.
8. Moshe Cohen, "A Bit of Peace," in Zim, *My Shalom*, 85.

intellectual, as delineated by Fernando Segovia in his presidential address. As a scholar in the Post-Global South of today, whose task is to explore the subjectivity and agency of subalterns,[9] I am convinced that biblical criticism that does not speak to the real needs of people, in this case children, is a luxury that the world can no longer afford.

The poems convey also the idea that war victimizes everyone. It is a truism that there are no heroes in war, only victims.[10] Even when society recognizes publicly the bravery displayed by combatants in countless armed conflicts by erecting monuments in their memory, still the sad reality is that everyone is a victim of that flesh-eating monster called War. The poem "I Don't Like Wars" says it best:

> I don't like wars
> They end up with monuments;
> I don't want battles to roar
> Even in neighboring continents.
>
> I like Spring
> Flowers producing
> Fields covered with green,
> The winds in the hills whistling.
>
> Drops of dew I love,
> The scent of jasmine as night cools,
> Stars in darkness above.
> And rain singing in pools.[11]

Matti Yosef was nine when he wrote this piece in 1974. His prophetic words have proven true time and again. Motionless, lifeless monuments dot the many battlefields of the world as a

9. Segovia, "Criticism in Critical Times," 19.

10. This quote is attributed to Ernest Hemingway who, in one of his letters to his parents written from a hospital bed at Milan and dated October 18, 1918, wrote, "There are no heroes in this war. We all offer our bodies and only a few are chosen, but it shouldn't reflect any special credit on those that are chosen. They are just the lucky ones." Usher, "There Are No Heroes."

11. Matti Yosef, "I Don't Like Wars," in Zim, *My Shalom*, 49.

sad reminder that war has not been, nor is, nor will ever be the solution to the problems of the human race. Contrary to that, as another child turned into a prophet reminded us two thousand years ago, "All who draw the sword will die by the sword" (Matt 26:52), because by so doing we perpetuate *ad infinitum* the cycle of violence.

Even people in uniform, those actively involved in waging war, want peace, says Frida Zeitelbah, age fourteen, in her poem "The Cry for Peace":

> I want to write
> About the cry for Peace
> Bursting from the bazooka's jaw
> At the foot of the uniformed figure;
> About the prayer for Peace
> You see in the eyes of officers
> In the War Room.[12]

This poem cuts deep into the fears and doubts of all those involved in warfare and is manifested in a fundamental question: Is it ever justifiable to kill another human being? This question has become utterly important lately, when we witness through social media the taking of human lives by fundamentalist extremist groups who perpetuate mass killings through human and car bombs, decapitation, and execution-style mass murders. Or by the indiscriminate bombing of the Gaza Strip by the Israeli army in disproportionate retaliation compared to the Palestinians' minor attacks. Or by the police, in excessive shows of force especially against minorities. Or simply by individuals who go on shooting rampages in schools, concerts, movie theaters, and places of work and worship. There is an undeclared war going on in many of the world's cities between gangs and drug cartels, in which hundreds of innocent people, especially children, lose their lives daily.[13]

---

12. Frida Zeitelbah, "The Cry for Peace," in Zim, *My Shalom*, 20.

13. The Gun Violence Archive has verified 934 deaths of children (under one year old up to seventeen years old) from gun violence as of September 2025. Gun Violence Archive, "GVA—10 Year Review."

War is that which takes my daddy away from me, says Elad Tabachnik, age eleven, in the poem "I Asked a Soldier":

> I turned to my mother asking:
> Peace, is it a positive or negative thing?
> My mother replied:
> Peace is joy and light!
> We need Peace, Shalom,
> So daddy will come home.[14]

On a similar vein, Efrat Shiler, age eleven, says in her poem "Blessed Art Thou" that when peace comes,

> Daddy will sit around and read his paper at ease,
> Instead of going up north to fight and freeze.
> And when Daddy from the war returns, then
> He'll never don his uniform again
> And on Purim I won't dress up like a soldier as before
> Because such things simply won't be anymore.[15]

It is hard to find a more poignant criticism of militarism than this! In spite of what is portrayed in the media about parents returning for a visit after months of service abroad, surprising their children who run to embrace them, we know that the price they have to pay for their parents' patriotic duty is family disruption, the fear of becoming orphans, which many do, the cessation of common activities such as going to school, and so on. All of this is part of their experience, as vividly reflected in the poem "Father and Son," written by an eleven-year-old:

> He has always wept and suffered without end,
> He wanted just this once
> To live again with his Dad
> Through those pleasant childhood days
> When they would walk together hand in hand,
> When a warm hand used to take him to school
> And he not wanting to part.

---

14. Elad Tabachnik, "I Asked a Soldier," in Zim, *My Shalom*, 13.
15. Efrat Shiler, "Blessed Art Thou," in Zim, *My Shalom*, 62.

Then came the war, and the hand was cut off.[16]

We also find similar ideas in the poem "Tomorrow," written by an eight-year-old:

> Tomorrow, tomorrow on Peace Day
> There'll be no orphans anymore,
> . . . .
> Tomorrow, when Peace comes,
> We won't waste money on arms
> We'll buy more cows for our farms.[17]

And in the poem "I Am Peace," Baruh Ron, age eight, expresses the profound insight that humans are born for peace, not for war:

> I am Peace, and Peace is me
> A human being—that's me
> Born for Peace.
> Disturb me not you clanging metals
> Of guns and armor plates
> Of planes taking off to battle
> Because Peace—that's me.[18]

At the end, all this sad state of affairs has been a pity, says Idan Brayer in his poem "A Pity":

> A pity, a pity, all this has been
> So let's forget and start again.[19]

In his book *Tomorrow's Child*, Rubem Alves gives us a powerful insight into the world of children. He says that the nature of this world is play. Children play; they create their own world with rules and roles defined by them in which they are both actors and authors of the script. As they play, they exchange roles between them. Nothing is permanent, everything is temporary, and by the end of the day they are ready to start again a new game. Alves says that "in play, each day begins with grace, not law. Every night is a moment of forgetting. Man must begin again. The adult world, by the fact that it preserves today

---

16. Amit Tal, "Father and Son," in Zim, *My Shalom*, 50.

17. Vardit Fertouk, "Tomorrow," in Zim, *My Shalom*, 88.

18. Baruh Ron, "I Am Peace," in Zim, *My Shalom*, 18.

19. Idan Brayer, "A Pity," in Zim, *My Shalom*, 61.

what was organized yesterday, never forgets. And therefore, never forgives. It is cruel."[20] It is this cruelty that has invented and preserved war to the expense of children's futures. There is no future for children in this world because sooner or later they are forced to become adults. They lose their joy, the pleasure of playing, and become enslaved; their imagination—dwarfed by laws and regulations—cannot give birth to anything; and their hopes and dreams are gone forever.

The world these children envision is certainly one that has never been experienced in history, and in that sense, it belongs to the realm of eschatology. It shares with biblical eschatology a tenacious, though sometimes skeptical, understanding of God's role in history. It holds in tension both assurance of deliverance and acceptance of the present reality of war, faith and fear, hope and despair. They are utopian, but, says Alves, they are not irrational products of consciousness. They are the voice of life itself. And in that regard he quotes Tillich as saying, "Utopias participate in truth. To deny them is thus a dangerous artifice, because in this negation one would be simply overcoming the truth that they hide."[21]

What do we learn about war from these poems? First of all, war is a sin, always. It victimizes everyone in such a way that there are no heroes, only victims. It ends up with wreaths and monuments, sad and lifeless reminders of the horrors of war. It divides families and makes orphans out of children. And it negates the basic essence of humans—namely, that of being born for peaceful coexistence.

EXTREME POVERTY

The second theme that I want to explore is that of extreme poverty, which manifests itself, among other things, in homelessness and substance and sexual abuse. In 2007 a turning point in the history of the world took place: more people live now in cities than in

20. Alves, *Tomorrow's Child*, 98.
21. Alves, *Tomorrow's Child*, 108.

rural areas. As a consequence, the city has produced a culture of its own where certain situations, deemed before as negative, are now seen as normal. An example of this is the existence of slums and the depressing reality of homelessness,[22] something that both Argentine and Palestinian children have in common.

There are eight thousand homeless people in Buenos Aires, half of whom are children, and a report by UNICEF says that there are fifty-four thousand children homeless in the Gaza Strip.[23] In both cases homelessness is the byproduct of extreme poverty.

In Argentina, poverty was at 40.6 percent in the first half of 2021, reaching 11.7 million people in urban agglomerations across the country. Extreme poverty was also on the rise, with 10.7 percent of the population now classified as destitute. Life in the shantytowns (*villas miseria*) of Buenos Aires is a clear sign of this reality, only to be outshone by life in the streets, under bridges and underpasses, on the benches of public squares, or in abandoned train stations. But during the first quarter of 2025 the poverty rate has dropped to 31.7 percent.[24]

> [In Palestine,] 2.5 million people (a little over half the population) including more than 1 million children are in need of humanitarian assistance. Almost one-third of Palestinian families live below the poverty line. . . . Unemployment rates are high: 32.4 percent across the State of Palestine—53.7 percent in the Gaza Strip, one of the highest rates in the world, with unemployment reaching 60 percent of youth in the Gaza Strip, where 80 percent of the population relies on some form of humanitarian assistance. Coping mechanisms are eroding fast, with some children and families resorting to negative strategies like school drop-out, child labor, substance abuse, and early marriage.[25]

22. Bazzell, *Urban Ecclesiology.*

23. Rey, "Homelessness Rises"; UNICEF, "State of Palestine."

24. Lo Bianco and Bustamente, "Argentina Poverty."

25. UNICEF, *Children,* 3.

The description above comes from quantitative data concerning the impact of extreme poverty on people in general and children in particular. But this data, though helpful, is faceless, detached, objective, and cold. It represents the voice of the experts. I am more interested in knowing how poverty affects real people, and for that I now turn to the voices of the victims as conveyed by their poetry.

The poem "Chico de la Calle" (Street Kid), written by Oscar Garay, age fifteen, speaks of that reality:

> Street kid, cold and hungry
> Sleeping in that abandoned station
> Empty of trains.
>
> Everybody looks at you with contempt,
> No one seems to really like you
> They don't know that you only want
> To take a ride in the merry-go-round.
>
> How unjust is the world,
> How sad is life
> If you can't jump
> On the merry-go-round
> For only one ride
> Would give you back your dreams
> And happy again,
> You would be.[26]

The child poet/prophet sees the huge gap that exists between the rich and the poor in the city of Buenos Aires and denounces it in clear and poignant ways: happiness for this boy is a cheap ticket in the merry-go-round which can never be compared to a dinner in a restaurant or to a show in a movie theater. He realizes that this is unjust, unfair, and so he denounces it as such. By describing it with crude realism, he is acting in a similar way to the prophets in ancient Israel who incited people to social change based on obedience to God's commandments. Typical of this idea is Mic 6:8:

---

26. Oscar Garay, "Chico de la Calle"; my translation.

He has told you, O mortal, what is good;
and what does the LORD require of you
but to do justice, and to love kindness,
and to walk humbly with your God? (Mic 6:8)

Life in the streets is tough, ruthless, and inhuman. The absolute absence of shelter makes people vulnerable and dependent on
others' pity and generosity. This is especially true when it comes
to children. An estimated four thousand homeless children popu-
late the streets of Buenos Aires, trying to earn a *peso* by offering
to clean the windshield of cars at red lights, improvising a jug-
gling act in front of pedestrians, or just asking for a *limosna* (alm),
which many times ends up in the hands of a drug dealer.[27] As I said
before, substance abuse and sexual exploitation represent some of
the most pervasive and damaging effects of extreme poverty on
the lives of children. The poem "La Droga" (Drugs), written also
by Oscar Garay, speaks about one of these realities, drug addiction:

Drugs separate you from the ones that you love
Nothing is important, nothing is worthwhile
They manipulate and control your mind
You're not even aware, you can't open your eyes
They kill you, slowly but surely.[28]

Sexual abuse and exploitation, as well as domestic violence,
are recurring problems in the *villas miseria*, prompted by crammed
living conditions, unemployment, and general frustration due to a
lack of a viable future for the families that live there. Children of
both sexes are usually the victims, the scapegoats, of such a situation, which generates unwanted pregnancies in girls as young as
twelve years old or their exploitation as sex workers.

27. One of the most popular drugs is called "Paco," made up of cocaine
residue, industrial solvents, and rat poison. It is smoked like crack and is said
to be fifty times stronger than cocaine. The effect is immediate but short-lived
(as little as twenty seconds), and it can lead to addiction in a very short time,
being much more addictive than heroin or crack. The Argentine government
estimates that in some shantytowns, as many as half of the young men between
the ages of thirteen and thirty are addicted. Bispuri, "Paco."

28. Oscar Garay, "La Droga"; my translation.

The poem "Yo Quisiera Ser un Ada"[29] (I Would Like to Be a Fairy) describes a world of sadness, suffering, hunger, alcohol, and drugs. The author wants to rescue young people from the allure of substance abuse and make them into true human beings. She goes on to plea for children by saying that were she a fairy, she would defend them from injustices, hunger, and poverty. She does not mention the by-products of these social ills, but she does not have to because, probably, she has experienced them firsthand. That is why she wants young people to be "hombres de verdad," (true men).

> I would like to be a fairy
> To be able to
> change the world
> So, instead of tears, hunger and suffering
> There would be peace, love, and happiness.
> I would like to be a fairy
> To be able to save young people
> From alcohol and drugs
> So they can become people of worth and truth.
> That is why I ask God from the bottom of my heart
> To change the world and to give us his blessing.[30]

The Three-Layered Context: Immediate Context, Regional Context, and World Context

Every given poem has an inner core which reflects the child's subjectivity affected by their social location. This social location, which is varied and fluctuating, is different for each child and accumulates in the poetry as layers of meaning. The first layer is provided by the immediate context in which the child is immersed in, be

29. The title of the poem already shows the social location of the author. "Ada" is written without "h," which is the proper spelling of the word. It may be a common mistake, or it may reflect that the author did not have access to good education due to her place of residence, the slums.

30. The poem's author wished to remain anonymous. "Yo Quisiera Ser un Ada"; my translation.

this the family or the lack of it, exemplified by homelessness. The second layer comes from the larger culture where this takes place, the region of the world where the child lives (South America, the Middle East, Africa, etc.). And there is a third "macro" layer: the global capitalist system, which affects differently each region and culture. Therefore, when you read a poem, you "open" a wealth of meaning prompted by this multilayered reality.[31]

In the preceding pages, the poems "I Asked a Soldier," "Blessed Art Thou," "Father and Son," and "La Droga," as they address issues related to family and friends, belong to the first layer. The poems "Prayer," "When Peace Will Finally Come," "Tomorrow," "A Pity," and "Chico de la Calle," focusing on the larger culture where their authors are embedded, in this case Israel/Palestine and Argentina, belong to the second layer. And the poems "A Bit of Peace," "I Don't Like Wars," "The Cry for Peace," and "Yo Quisiera Ser un Ada" subscribe to the idea of peace in a broader, universal sense. That is the third layer.

We can see an analogous division by layers in the Gospel of Mark. The first is provided by the immediate context in which the evangelist is immersed—namely, his community during the Jewish-Roman war—the second comes from the broader Palestinian culture, and the third is represented by the Roman Empire, the "macro" layer. Therefore, when you read the Gospel you "open" a wealth of meaning prompted by this multilayered reality. In this book I am attempting to explore the intertextuality between children's poetry and the biblical text as well as the intersubjectivity between its authors.[32]

---

31. I would contend that the same thing happens when one reads an ancient biblical text, for example the Gospel of Mark.

32. Here I am aware of Kristeva's criticism of the very notion of intersubjectivity (see Beal, "Ideology and Intertextuality," 30).

Chapter 3

War and Extreme Poverty
as Themes in Mark

WE START WITH THE QUESTION, How did war and extreme poverty affect the children of the Markan community? I assume as the social context for the writing of the Gospel of Mark the Jewish-Roman war of 66–70 CE.[1] And I also assume a situation of occupation and extreme poverty. Given this scenario, the various children portrayed in the Gospel of Mark are all undergoing some kind of oppression: Jairus's daughter is sick and then dies (Mark 5:39–41); the daughter of the Syrophoenician woman is demon possessed (7:24–30); the boy whose father comes to the disciples for healing is also demon possessed (9:17–29); the little children brought to Jesus for blessing are in need of physical protection (Jesus took them in his arms: 9:36–37, 10:13–16); the daughter of Herodias is used by her parents to fulfill their own power-driven agendas (6:17–29); children are victims of their parents' betrayal and are put to death by the authorities (13:12a); and children are subject to ideological manipulation and denounce their parents, which sends them also to death (13:12b).

If Mark writes the story of Jesus informed by his own community's situation, then it is fair to assume that the war had

---

1. Myers, *Binding the Strong Man*, 64–69; Hooker, *Mark*, 8, 299–300, 302–3; Brown, *Introduction to the New Testament*, 127.

produced a sharp division in the family unity, with children being both subjects and forced agents of violent death. The family, being the basic unit of the Greco-Roman world, was essential to keep the harmony of the whole society. If it was disrupted, or divided in any way, it created chaos and confusion and constituted a threat to the imperial order. The Romans tried to prevent anything from upsetting the fabric of society to the point of even provoking the fragmentation of those family units that they perceived as troublesome or deviant, groups whose internal structure was at odds with the imperial model of patronage. One such group was the Jesus movement.[2] As mentioned earlier, the enmity between parents and children mentioned by Mark in 13:12 is a traditional apocalyptic motif (see Mic 7:6; 2 Esd 6:24),[3] but it probably happened among first-century believers especially during the time of the Jewish-Roman war. It is not impossible that children were used as informants by the authorities in order to break the family's allegiance to the movement.[4] Judas seems to have played that role in the Gospel narrative (Mark 3:19; 14:10, 43–46).

The Jewish-Roman war also brought about extreme poverty, with its concomitant side effects of sickness that sometimes led to premature death, demonic possession (today we might call it mental illness) that produced terrible oppression and suffering, and the marginality and abandonment of children by adults when they joined the Jesus movement (see above).

2. It has been noticed by many that the model of family that Jesus has in mind lacks a father, the absolute source of authority in those days (Mark 10:30).

3. The disintegration of family life due to a lack of trust among its members informs Micah's oracle. He describes family life under the threat of the Assyrian invasion, painting a gloomy picture of betrayal, distrust, and plain enmity as people take sides in the approaching and inevitable fate of the nation.

4. For a description of the ancient and modern-day role of informants, including that of children, see Rich, "Use of Citizen Informants." See also Tamez, "Conflict in Mark," 108–9, where she talks about the role of the informant in the Colombian guerrilla war, something known as *sapeo*, "frogging," and which entails "the betrayal of someone for profit, or the act of being a longtime paid informant, obtaining information from any side."

But Mark's was a world of adults, as is ours. None of the major sociopolitical decisions made by the leaders of the world today are aimed specifically and purposefully at the betterment of children's lives. So, when improvements in children's lives do occur, they are due to the work of people who advocate for their rights and are able to make changes in the policies of their countries. But by and large this is done by the initiative of isolated groups of individuals, not governments. When countries go to war, for example, they do not consider how this would harm children and minorities. They engage in war for nationalistic, patriotic, and economic reasons, not for humanistic ones. Given this scenario, children are always victims, collateral damage, that forgotten part of humanity that needs continual advocacy on the part of aware individuals.

Was Mark then an advocate for children? It all depends on how one interprets the little ones of Mark 9:42 and what the function of verses 38–41 are. These verses seem to interrupt what could otherwise be considered a continuous narrative—namely, if verse 42 followed right after verse 37. If that is the case, then one can conclude that verses 36–37 and verses 42–48 are to be read together and that they represent a warning against pederasty (see above). The interpolation of verses 38–41[5] may have served the purpose of mitigating or denying the shameful behavior of some adults in the community by spiritualizing what was clearly a sexual misconduct into something that could be explained as a lack of tolerance for those who, though believing in Jesus, were not joining the community.

INTERSUBJECTIVITY: THE EVANGELIST AND THE CHILDREN

The issue of systemic violence, both physical and psychological, is the backdrop against which Mark writes his Gospel. The first

5. Matthew 12:30 states the saying negatively: "Whoever is not with me is against me, and whoever does not gather with me scatters." Luke 9:50 follows Mark and uses it in a positive way: "Do not stop him; for whoever is not against you is for you."

is exercised by the Roman Empire through its minions: Pontius Pilate (against Jesus) and Herod (against John the Baptist).[6] The other issue is abuse, both sexual and economic. Sexual abuse is not clearly stated but can be deduced from an informed reading of Mark 9:38–41 (see below). Economic abuse is seen in the case of the poor widow at the temple (Mark 12:41–44), the hemorrhaging woman of Mark 5:25–34, the peasants that constitute the background for the parables of the kingdom, etc.

Violence against children is not one of Mark's main concerns but one that is secondary to his major aim of announcing God's reign. That is why many believe that his representation of children is merely circumstantial. But underneath his depiction of children, there is a recollection of Jesus' own attitude toward them. This recollection, these memories, came from the oral traditions that underscored the Gospel, which had been circulating in the community for nearly a generation. Mark seems to have been the first one to put them into writing because his version of Jesus' life is followed closely by Matthew and Luke. They agree with Mark in many themes, one of them being the way Jesus viewed and treated children.

In this work we are concerned with the evangelist's, not Jesus', voice. To know exactly what Jesus' attitude toward children was is impossible because the oral traditions preserved in the Gospels have already been shaped by the theological concerns of their authors, prompted by the needs of their communities. The relationship between history and theology is a known conundrum in contemporary Gospel studies, one which I am not addressing in this work. I am only recognizing the problem and affirming the likelihood that when we see Jesus interacting with children, it is probably a true historical occurrence preserved by the tradition but filtered through the ideology of the evangelist.

6. One could argue that Jesus also used violence during the temple riot, but this violence was not aimed at people's lives, but it was meant to disrupt what he considered taking advantage of the sacrificial system in order to benefit their economic gains.

With a little imagination, based on known historical facts about the social world of first-century Palestine, and with a due recognition of the obvious differences between that world and ours, it is possible to say that Jesus had many things in common with the children whose poems are the subject of this work: he lived in occupied Palestine, under social unrest, in a poor region of the country (Galilee), and envisioned a new society, the kingdom of God, the kingdom of shalom. He experienced the Roman occupation of Palestine and was a witness to the presence of rebel groups operating in the countryside, not unlike what Palestinian children in Gaza and the West Bank experience today. Also, living at a mere subsistence level in Nazareth—a poor and insignificant hamlet in Galilee—he knew poverty firsthand, "unfiltered," as Jorge Luis Borges suggests in one of his works.[7] In this regard he shared the experience of so many Latin American children of whom those living in La Ciudad Oculta (The Hidden City) are but an example. Therefore, Jesus' experience of occupation and extreme poverty brings the Jesus of history existentially and emotionally close to the children of Palestine and Argentina, and makes him a kindred spirit who would have understood these children's predicament. Of course, we know all of that "through" Mark's rendition of it, as we already pointed out, since there are no historical records about the life of Jesus except by a few references in the literature of the time, both Greco-Roman and Jewish.[8] Therefore, we have no other

7. "To be poor implies a more immediate possession of reality, a charging against the first rough taste of things, knowledge that the rich seem to lack, as if everything would reach them unfiltered." Borges, *Obras Completas*, 129; my translation.

8. Greco-Roman sources: Pliny the Younger, governor of Bithynia, writing to emperor Trajan, asks about how to deal with Christians in his province (*Letters* 10.96–97) around 112 CE; Suetonius, a Roman historian, talks about riots instigated by one named "Chrestus" (*Claudius* 25) around 114 CE; and Tacitus, a Roman historian, writes in his *Annals* that Nero blamed the Christians for the burning of Rome (*Annals* 15.44). He also gives the first reference to Jesus as having been executed under Pontius Pilate (115 CE). Jewish sources: Josephus, writing during and after the Jewish revolt of 66–71 CE, mentions Jesus as being the brother of James (*Antiquities* 20.9.1) and as being a wise man, teacher, and miracle worker, crucified by Pilate, and followed by many until Josephus's very

option but to trust the oral traditions as conveying at least a semblance of who Jesus was.

Earlier in this book I contended that the poetry I am analyzing can be treated as prophetic utterances and its authors as prophets. In that regard, it is important to notice that Jesus described himself as a prophet (see Mark 6:4) and used poetry to bring his message across. It is true that his sayings, aphorisms, riddles, and the like do not look like poetry because they do not have rhyme; but they have rhythm, and that qualifies them as poetry.[9] Like the children of Israel/Palestine and the Hidden City of Buenos Aires, Jesus, the child turned prophet, used poetry as a medium for his prophetic proclamation.

day (*Antiquities* 18.3.3).

9. Robert H. Stein affirms that the poetry of Jesus is to be found not in its rhyme but in its rhythmic balance (Stein, "Biblical Hermeneutics"). Examples of this rhythmic balance abound throughout the Gospels. Mark 3:24–25 is one of them: "If a kingdom is divided against itself, that kingdom cannot stand. And if a house is divided against itself, that house cannot stand." Also, Luke 6:27–28: "But to you who are listening I say: Love your enemies, do good to those who hate you, bless those who curse you, pray for those who mistreat you." Furthermore, the Sermon on the Mount in general (Matt 5:1—7:27) and the Beatitudes in particular (Matt 5:3–11) constitute some of the clearest examples of this kind of poetry. Borges, *Obras Completas*, 129.

Chapter 4

Envisioning the Kingdom
and the Poems as Stories

RUBEM ALVES, IN HIS book *The Poet, the Warrior, the Prophet*, talks about stories and says that they have power "only because their past and distance are metaphors for the here and now. They never actually happened, so that they can happen always, everywhere."[1] He is referring specifically to the mystery of the incarnation, but I suggest that it can also be applied to other themes, such as the kingdom of God. We can also say about the kingdom that it will never actually happen, so it can happen always and everywhere.

As a story, the kingdom happens only in literature, never in history per se. That is, it is not a historical reality but more an idea that impacts history by changing it. If one accepts the fact that everything in the Bible is a literary and ideological construction, then the kingdom of God is part of that construction. One of the most important aspects of that construction is that it never materializes completely because if it does it loses its liberating force, it is trapped in the contingency of a specific place and time forever. That is not what the kingdom of God is all about. Rather, the kingdom is a hope, a dream that is envisioned not as a theocracy but more as a democracy in the traditional sense of the term—that is, the government of the people that translates into the practice and

1. Alves, *Poet*, 74.

principles of social equality. Since this has never been achieved, it remains a hope, a utopia. It belongs to the realm of eschatology, not history.

When the Bible narrates the events of the eschaton, the end of days when the kingdom of God will be established on earth, it does so as part of the whole story that the Bible is. Starting with the premise that everything in the Bible is literature that is being used by different authors to express their hope in God's liberating action, it helps us to de-historicize the kingdom and see it only as eschatological.

Now, where is the power of eschatology to be found? Certainly not in its historicity but in its non-historicity, in its openness to the future. How else can we explain the eschatological passages in the Bible that were used and reused to fit the needs of new generations of believers. Take for example those passages in Isaiah that talk about new heavens and new earth and how they were useful to the writer of Revelation to describe the new world he was envisioning. Eight hundred years had gone by, empires had risen and crumbled, and yet the words of the prophet were still relevant. The same can be said about the idea of the Son of Man, first developed in the book of Daniel, but reshaped and used later in 2 Esdras and 1 Enoch, only to be used again by Mark when he described Jesus as the Son of Man. There are other examples, but these should suffice to show the nature of the eschatological passages as that of being always susceptible to expansion, adaptation, and rereading. Today we would use the word "recycling." The eschatological events described in the Bible can never happen in history because history and eschatology are two different things. But they can, and they do, influence the present and envision the future. In that sense they can happen always and everywhere.

I would argue that the children's poems, because they tell a story, and a sad one at that, are eschatological in nature. The children envisioned something they had never seen before. It is like a story their parents tell them before they go to bed so they may be able to sleep without fear. One of the purposes of the kingdom as a story, or the poems as stories, is precisely that: to allow those who express it to be at peace in spite of it all. If one has to summarize the message of the kingdom and the message of the poems, it would be peace. But because peace is not a present reality, it then becomes an eschatological reality, something that impacts history without being historical, as we pointed out before. The kingdom, as well as the poems, can happen over and over again, always and everywhere. They are not tied to a specific historical context. For instance, we read the children's poems today, forty years after they were written, and we realize that they still have the same pertinency because peace—the kingdom—has not become part of our reality. In that sense these poems are utopian, and their authors are makers of utopias—prophets, as already suggested.

Therefore, the question remains: When will the kingdom happen? When will the present world give way to the world announced in the eschatological passages of the Bible and the poems? And the answer is never—and always. These writings will slowly produce a change of minds and of hearts until a new society, one in which peace is the norm and not the exception, will emerge. But it will be impossible to make a cause-and-effect connection between the passages/poems and the new reality because the new reality will be unconscious, even natural. When this happens, eschatology will not be necessary anymore until it is needed again by a new generation of disappointed humans.

Chapter 5

The Playground of Biblical Scholarship[1]

WHO CAN PLAY IN THE PLAYGROUND?

One could say that biblical scholarship is a sort of playground where scholars participate according to a set of rules. Traditionally, the gate to this playground has been the historical-critical method (HCM). This method (or methods), assuming the mantle of universality and scientific objectivity and neutrality, has imposed its findings on all people everywhere, regardless of culture and social location. It has been the gate to, but also the gatekeeper of, the academic world, and every individual who prized himself/herself as a serious scholar, myself included, had to enter the playground of New Testament studies through it. Once inside, we were guided by the official leaders of the field, usually North American and European scholars, to become part of the playground. The system was (and still is) very paternalistic and patriarchal since the majority of scholars were (and still are) white heterosexual males. Minoritized[2] scholars and their interpretive methods were not considered

1. In this section I will rely on my forthcoming article, "The Social Dimension of the Johannine 'I Am.'"

2. I want to make a distinction between *minority* and *minoritized*. The former understands people from the perspective of the dominant culture, seeing them as ancillary to it. The latter understands people from their own perspective, as those who recognize that their views, though legitimate, have been suppressed by the dominant culture and made inferior, *minor*.

serious. At the most, they were regarded as interesting rarities, but they remained marginal and unimportant because they did not subscribe to the historical-critical method's claim of being "scientific, value-neutral, and objective."[3]

These contextual methods, rather than concentrating on a positivistic analysis of the text and the historical situation in which it was produced, consider the text as a rhetorical construct, trying to understand how it functions in the lives of people.[4] They do not concentrate as much on exegesis as they do on hermeneutics, not as much on the apparently value-neutral nature of the biblical text as they do on its highly ideological function. And, especially, they emphasize the role of the reader in the construction of meaning, foregrounding the social location of the scholar as the primary tool in the interpretive task.

Even though these methods have been in existence for quite some time, they still remain marginal in some academic circles. They constitute a new paradigm, termed by Fernando Segovia as cultural studies: "This new development posits instead a very different construct, the flesh-and-blood reader: always positioned and interested; socially and historically conditioned and unable to transcend such conditions—to attain a sort of asocial and ahistorical nirvana—not only with respect to socioeconomic class but also with regard to the many other factors that make up human identity."[5]

Originally, the HCM developed out of the need to liberate biblical interpretation from the dogmatic constraints imposed by the church. It became a tool in the hands of secularists, and as such it began to be distinguished from the church's own tools to the point of both becoming separate, with no or few connections between them. But the church, being historically the mother of the academy, couldn't forget her child, so she allowed academic pursuits to dictate its interpretive responsibility. And since the HCM was the main tool

---

3. Schüssler Fiorenza, *Democratizing Biblical Studies*, 31.
4. Schüssler Fiorenza, *Democratizing Biblical Studies*, 71.
5. Segovia, "They Began to Speak," 32.

used in academia, it also became the main tool used by the church's exegetes, thus creating the scenario described above.

Today we still recognize the fact that the field of biblical studies needs to continue to produce the knowledge that nurtures the church—and sometimes I get the feeling that the field of biblical studies and the church have completely different agendas—and to shepherd those who want to serve the church. Using the imagery shown in John 10:16, it will have to make room for the other sheep the Johannine Jesus is talking about in this passage: "I have other sheep that do not belong to this fold. I must bring them also, and they will listen to my voice. So there will be one flock, one shepherd." Changing the image of fold to that of playground, this metaphor seems to imply that when it comes to reading the text, a diversity of interpreters and their methods—the "other sheep"— is preferred because, in the end, this diversity does not affect the unity of the field/fold/playground but rather contributes to it, ensuring that it remains truthful to its original purpose of elucidating the meaning(s) of the biblical text for a contemporary situation. Rather than adhering to the dichotomous idea of exegesis and application still espoused by the traditional methodology, what we have now is a series of multilayered approaches, or readings, that engage the text from a variety of perspectives, all of them necessary and legitimate, carrying equal authority,[6] all of them part of the playground of biblical studies.

Debunking the assumptions of the HCM is part of serving as open gates and gentle shepherds to a new community of scholars who are coming into the field/fold/playground of biblical studies from many different countries, cultures, and social locations. All of these scholars make important and relevant contributions to the construction of knowledge. We do not want the HCM to go away, to simply disappear, because there is much to be learned from it. But we want it to stop being the gatekeeper, the "bouncer," of the field/fold/playground of biblical studies. It should remain what it is, another valid method, but not the only one. In Johannine language, it should be part of the sheep, of the fold, but not the

6. Patte, *Ethics*, 40.

shepherd itself. To use a quote from Wayne A. Meeks, "Historical exegesis would relinquish its modernist role as umpire, no longer authorized simply to declare contemporizing interpretations 'safe' or 'out.' Instead, it would act as a kind of *advocatus diaboli*, standing up for the past in a dialogue between Then and Now."[7]

I believe that the study of any biblical text should have praxis as its final goal. But since praxis is always contextual, the methods that contribute to it should also be contextual. Biblical exegesis in Latin America was changed forever with the birth of liberation theology. A new cadre of scholars followed the path opened by Gustavo Gutiérrez, slowly detaching themselves from the constraints of the HCM and making use of the many methodologies available to them in the secular world. They brought to the analysis of the Bible different questions shaped by their different sociopolitical realities, a predicament not shared by the traditional European scholars. With time, liberation theology itself was challenged and changed from the inside by people who had not been in the original "first wave" of the movement—namely, women, sexual minorities, and people of color—and so the "founding fathers" had to bring into their range of vision the concerns brought about by these groups, to which I would like to add children.[8] The church in Latin America had to adapt to this new way of reading the text, and this influenced everything the church did—its liturgy, preaching and teaching, organization, position on social issues and on women's ministries, and the like.

THE CONTRIBUTION OF CHILDREN TO THE PLAYGROUND OF BIBLICAL INTERPRETATION

Children are not biblical scholars. They are natural, intuitive interpreters of reality, and they do that through their creativity seen in play and art. It is our responsibility as biblical scholars to acknowledge their vision of the world as a tool, as an instrument that can

7. Meeks, "Trusting an Unpredictable God," 119.

8. See here Vena, "Lectura del evangelio," and Sánchez Cetina, "Niño tiene la palabra."

break open the text to new interpretive possibilities. It is a new social location, a new culture—that of children.

I have already advanced in this work the possibility of considering these children as prophets and their poems as poetic prophecy, similar to what we find in the Bible among certain prophets. And this begs the question, What is the relationship between poetry and prophesy? To answer it we have to turn to the work of William Franke posted online.[9] His analysis of this issue is extremely sophisticated, and much of it does not apply to our concerns, but some of his more general conclusions may prove to be instructive.

Franke says that in the history and prehistory of human societies, poets, prophets, and seers have been used as synonyms. Their respective activities overlap to such an extent that prophets and poets tend to amalgamate in many of their functions and modalities. In the Bible, the Hebrew word *nabi* for "prophet" means "bubbling forth, as from a fountain," suggesting the creative fecundity of verbal imagination.[10] Examples of this are Amos, Isaiah, Elisha, and Ezekiel, who produced parables, proverbs, and even love songs. Yet, not everyone agrees with this. In fact, a certain ideology running through the Bible tries to drive a wedge between God-inspired prophecy and humanly created poems. But in primitive cultures, before the roles of prophet or poet were identified, a shaman or a wizard embodied both ideas: religious revelation and creative imagination and invention.

In modern cultures, theological revelation and poetry are typically seen as two separate activities and, at times, are even regarded as opposed to each other. As Franke says, "The two still need to be understood together as reciprocal and symbiotic in their origins, aims, and purposes. . . . Poetry and prophecy together comprise the common matrix of some of the oldest and most fundamental modes of expression of humanity across cultures."[11] When the Hebrew prophets utilized poetry to convey their prophetic message, they were tapping unconsciously into this common

9. Franke, "Poetry."
10. Franke, "Poetry."
11. Franke, "Poetry."

matrix. The same can be said of these children's poems: they are prophetic even though their authors do not realize it. But we do. We make them prophetic; the children do not. Our rereading of the poems makes them hermeneutical tools to read the biblical text. That has been our aim throughout this book. It is now up to the readers to assess its validity and pertinence.

CONCLUSION

Exploring the Hermeneutical Possibilities When Examining Two Texts That Seem Not to Be Related

As I said in the introduction, my purpose in this book has been to bring into dialogue two communities: one hypothetical, the other real. For the former, I have used a name common among scholars: the Markan community. For the latter, I have invented a name: the community of the playground. These two communities talk to each other through the texts they have produced, thus constituting an extended exercise in intertextuality in which every text is an intersection of other texts that are themselves intersections, overlaps, and collisions, without center or boundaries (see above, page 2). In fact, this book is an attempt at exploring the hermeneutical possibilities of two texts that seem not to be related, and it does so independently from the tyranny of the historical-critical method.

Bibliography

Alamy. "Childs Sarcophagus Stock Photos and Images." https://www.alamy.com/stock-photo/childs-sarcophagus.html?sortBy=relevant.

Alves, Rubem. *The Poet, the Warrior, the Prophet*. London: SCM, 2002.

————. *Tomorrow's Child: Imagination, Creativity, and the Rebirth of Culture*. London: SCM, 1972.

Archard, David. *Children: Rights and Childhood*. London: Routledge, 1993.

Attridge, Harold W., ed. *The Harper Collins Study Bible: New Revised Standard Version, with the Apocryphal/Deuterocanonical Books; Student Edition*. Rev. and updated ed. San Francisco: HarperSanFrancisco, 1989.

Bazzell, Pascal D. *Urban Ecclesiology: Gospel of Mark, Familia Dei and a Filipino Community Facing Homelessness*. London: T&T Clark, 2015.

Beal, Timothy K. "Ideology and Intertextuality: Surplus of Meaning and Controlling the Means of Production." In *Reading Between Texts: Intertextuality and the Hebrew Bible*, edited by Danna Nolan Fewell. Louisville: Westminster John Knox, 1992.

Bispuri, Valerio. "Paco: A Drug Story." Visa pour l'Image. https://www.visapourlimage.com/en/festival/exhibitions/paco-une-histoire-de-drogue.

Borg, Marcus J., and John Dominic Crossan. *The First Paul: Reclaiming the Radical Visionary Behind the Church's Conservative Icon*. New York: HarperOne, 2009.

Borges, Jorge Luis. *Obras Completas 1: 1923–1949*. 5th ed. Buenos Aires: Emecé, 2010.

Brown, Raymond E. *An Introduction to the New Testament*. New Haven: Yale University Press, 1997.

Cohen, Shaye, ed. *The Jewish Family in Antiquity*. Atlanta: Scholars Press, 1993.

Cooper, John. *The Child in Jewish History*. Northvale, NJ: Jason Aronson, 1996.

Ellis, Wesley W. "'God Was with the Child': A Childist Hermeneutic for the Interpretation of Scripture." *Berkeley Journal of Religion and Theology* 2 (2016) 108–22.

Flynn, Shawn W. *Children in the Bible and the Ancient World: Comparative and Historical Methods in Reading Ancient Children.* Studies in the History of the Ancient Near East. London: Routledge, 2019.

Flynn, Shawn W., and Kristine Garroway. "Children in the Ancient Middle East Were Valued and Vulnerable—Not Unlike Children Today." The Conversation, Dec. 12, 2019. https://theconversation.com/children-in-the-ancient-middle-east-were-valued-and-vulnerable-not-unlike-children-today-120490.

Franke, William. "Poetry, Prophecy, and Theological Revelation." *Oxford Research Encyclopedia of Religion,* May 9, 2016. https://doi.org/10.1093/acrefore/9780199340378.013.205.

Grassi, Joseph A. *Children's Liberation: A Biblical Perspective.* Collegeville, MN: Liturgical, 1991.

Gun Violence Archive. "GVA—10 Year Review." Last updated September 27, 2025. https://www.gunviolencearchive.org/.

Hooker, Morna D. *The Gospel According to Saint Mark.* Peabody, MA: Hendrickson, 1992.

Human Rights Watch. "Children Used as Soldiers in Most Major Conflicts." Nov. 16, 2004. http://www.hrw.org/news/2004/11/16/children-used-soldiers-most-major-conflicts.

James, Allison, and Alan Prout, eds. *Constructing and Reconstructing Childhood: New Directions in the Sociology of Childhood.* New York: Falmer, 1990.

Jenkins, Henry, ed. *The Children's Culture Reader.* New York: New York University Press, 1998.

Jenks, Chris. *Childhood.* 2nd ed. London: Routledge, 2005.

Jones, Sam. "Boko Haram: Soaring Numbers of Children Used in Suicide Attacks, Says Unicef." *The Guardian,* Apr. 12, 2016. http://www.theguardian.com/global-development/2016/apr/12/children-suicide-attacks-boko-haram-unicef-nigeria.

Koetje, Jeffrey. "'We're His Damn Kids, Too, You Know!' Childhood, Children, Tragedy and Hope in God's Neighborhood." Unpublished paper, May 8, 2003.

Kristeva, Julia. *Revolution in Poetic Language.* Translated by Margaret Waller. New York: Columbia University Press, 1984.

———. *Desire in Language: A Semiotic Approach to Literature and Art.* Edited by Leon S. Roudiez. Translated by Thomas Gora et al. New York: Columbia University Press, 1980.

Lao Tzu. *Tao Te Ching.* Translated by Stephen Mitchell. New York: Harper & Row, 1988.

Loader, William. *Sexuality and the Jesus Tradition.* Grand Rapids: Eerdmans, 2005.

Lo Bianco, Miguel, and Juan Carlos Bustamente. "Argentina Poverty Levels Slide, Though Many Still Feel the Pinch." Reuters, last updated Mar. 31, 2025. https://www.reuters.com/world/americas/poverty-hit-argentines-rummage-food-even-economic-outlook-improves-2025-03-31/.

Malina, Bruce, and Richard Rohrbaugh. *Social Science Commentary on the Synoptic Gospels.* 2nd ed. Minneapolis: Fortress, 2003.

McFague, Sallie. *The Body of God: An Ecological Theology.* Philadelphia: Fortress, 1993.

Meeks, Wayne A. "On Trusting an Unpredictable God: A Hermeneutical Meditation on Romans 9–11." In *Faith and History: Essays in Honor of Paul W. Meyer,* edited by John T. Carroll et al. Atlanta: Scholars Press, 1990.

Mills, Charles W. *The Racial Contract.* Ithaca: Cornell University Press, 1997.

Murphy, A. James. *Kids and Kingdom: The Precarious Presence of Children in the Synoptic Gospels.* Eugene, OR: Pickwick, 2013.

Myers, Ched. *Binding the Strong Man.* Maryknoll, NY: Orbis, 2008.

Nathan, Geoffrey S. *The Family in Late Antiquity: The Rise of Christianity and the Endurance of Tradition.* London: Routledge, 2000.

Okure, Teresa. "Children in Mark." In *Mark: Texts @ Contexts,* edited by Nicole Wilkinson Duran et al. Minneapolis: Fortress, 2010.

Patte, Daniel. *Ethics of Biblical Interpretation: A Reevaluation.* Louisville: Westminster John Knox, 1995.

Regents of the University of Michigan. "Archaeologies of Childhood." https://exhibitions.kelsey.lsa.umich.edu/archaeologies-of-childhood/childhood.php.

Rey, Debora. "Homelessness Rises in Argentina's Capital amid Crisis." AP News, Mar. 28, 2019. https://apnews.com/article/financial-markets-caribbean-ap-top-news-argentina-international-news-acaae15e2133488aa41c8bef7a1f6147.

Rich, Mark M. "Use of Citizen Informants." New World War. http://www.newworldwar.org/informants.htm.

Sánchez Cetina, Edesio. "El niño tiene la palabra." In Voth and Barrera, *Servir, Sentir, Discernir,* 13–21.

Schüssler Fiorenza, Elisabeth. *Democratizing Biblical Studies: Toward an Emancipatory Educational Space.* Louisville: Westminster John Knox, 2009.

Segovia, Fernando F. "And They Began to Speak in Other Tongues." In *Decolonizing Biblical Studies: A View from the Margins,* 3–32. Maryknoll, NY: Orbis, 2000.

———. "Criticism in Critical Times: Reflections on Vision and Task." *Journal of Biblical Literature* 134 (2015) 6–29.

Sinha, Priyanka. "Children of Syria." Humanium. https://www.humanium.org/en/syria/.

Somerville, John. *The Rise and Fall of Childhood.* Beverly Hills, CA: Sage, 1982.

Stein, Robert. "Biblical Hermeneutics—Lesson 17." BiblicalTraining.org. https://www.biblicaltraining.org/learn/institute/nt510-biblical-hermeneutics/nt510-17-hermeneutics-for-poetry-part-1.

Tamez, Elsa. "The Conflict in Mark: A Reading from the Armed Conflict in Colombia." In *Mark: Texts @ Contexts*, edited by Nicole Wilkinson Duran et al. Minneapolis: Fortress, 2011.

UNICEF. *Children in the State of Palestine.* Nov. 2018. https://www.unicef.org/sop/media/341/file.

———. "More Than Half of Ukraine's Children Displaced After One Month of War." Mar. 24, 2022. https://www.unicef.org/press-releases/more-half-ukraines-children-displaced-after-one-month-war.

Usher, Shaun. "There Are No Heroes in This War." Letters of Note, Oct. 18, 2023. https://news.lettersofnote.com/p/there-are-no-heroes-in-this-war.

Vena, Osvaldo D. "(The) Blessing (of) the Little Ones." *Apuntes* 26.4 (2006) 143–51.

———. "Una lectura del evangelio de Marcos a través de la poesía de niñas y niños oprimidos." In Voth and Barrera, *Servir, Sentir, Discernir*, 23–43.

———. "The Social Dimension of the Johannine 'I Am' Sayings." In *John: Texts @ Contexts*, edited by Nicole Duran et al. Minneapolis: Fortress, forthcoming.

Voth, Estaban, and Juan José Barrera, eds. *Servir, Sentir, Discernir: Ensayos bíblicos en homenaje Edesio Sánchez-Cetina.* Buenos Aires, AMAX Ediciones, 2019.

Wall, John. "Childhood Studies, Hermeneutics, and Theological Ethics." *The Journal of Religion* 86.4 (2006) 523–48.

Wikipedia. "William Franke (Philosopher)." Wikimedia Foundation, last updated June 19, 2025. https://en.wikipedia.org/wiki/William_Franke_(philosopher).

Witherington, Ben, III. *The Gospel of Mark: A Socio-Rhetorical Commentary.* Grand Rapids: Eerdmans, 2008.

Zim, Jacob, ed. *My Shalom My Peace: Paintings and Poems by Jewish and Arab Children.* Poems selected by Uriel Ofek. Translated by Dov Vardi. Tel Aviv: Sabra; New York: McGraw-Hill, 1975.

www.ingramcontent.com/pod-product-compliance
Lightning Source LLC
Chambersburg PA
CBHW052222090426
42741CB00010B/2635